TIME GENTLEME!

Lost pubs of Leek & the
Staffordshire Moorlands

Lindsey & Phillip Porter

Dialogue between
Mr. Sam Godwin & Mr. Harry Mee,
given in the Town Hall about thirty years ago.

"Sambo, I hear you are going to open a Menagerie in Leek."

"Yes, Mr. Johnson, I am going to turn all the Public-Houses into a Menagerie."

"What sort of animals have you Sambo?"

"I have a **Red Lion**, two **White Lions**, a **Sea Lion**, a **Black Lion**, a **Golden Lion**, a **Roe Buck**, and a **Unicorn**."

"I hear you have an Art Gallery in addition to the Menagerie."

"Yes, Mr. Johnson, as you go in on the left you will see a **King's Head**, a **Queen's Head**, a **Bull's Head**, a **Wilkes's Head**, a **Black's Head**, and a **Nag's Head**. The **Dog and Partridge** and the **Bird-in-Hand** will live together in **Union**, the **Black Swan**, and the **Swan with two necks** will sail together on the tranquil waters of the **Fountain**, while the two **Cocks** will pick up grain under the **Wheatsheaf**. Visitors to the Show will find every accommodation at the various Taverns, where there will be a plentiful supply of good old **Cheshire Cheese** and **Grapes** free, also the use of the **Bowling Green**. Those visitors who come by **Railway** will come by the **Churnet Valley**, and will see such sights as were never seen in the days of **Wellington** this side of the **Globe**. The **Flying Horse** and the **Dun Cow** will graze under the shady branches of the **Royal Oaks**. The **Jolly Sailor** will crack his sides with laughing at a **Green Man** talking to a **Quiet Woman**. The **Dyers' Arms** will juggle with the **Blue Ball** at night under the expanding wings of the **Spread Eagle**."

"Have you any distinguished patrons, Sambo?"

"Yes! I have **King William IV, Duke of York, Lord Raglan, Earl Grey** and **Wellington** who may be distinguished by wearing a **Moss Rose** in their buttonholes. The show will be held in the **Cattle Market**, there will be fodder for the cattle at the **Talbot**, the **Angel** will guard over the whole collection and when the band has played **Britannia**, **George** will lock up the show with the **Cross Keys**."

Extract from *The Leek News*, 1928.

LANDMARK COLLECTOR'S LIBRARY

TIME GENTLEMEN PLEASE

Lost pubs of Leek & the Staffordshire Moorlands

Lindsey & Phillip Porter

" BLACK'S HEAD."

Landmark Publishing

Published by

LANDMARK
Publishing Ltd ● ● ● ●

Ashbourne Hall, Cokayne Ave
Ashbourne, Derbyshire DE6 1EJ England
Tel: (01335) 347349 Fax: (01335) 347303
e-mail: landmark@clara.net
web site: www.landmarkpublishing.co.uk

ISBN: 1-84306-194-5

British Library Cataloguing in Publication Data: a catalogue
record for this book is available from the British Library.

Printed by Gutenburg Press Ltd, Malta

Design & reproduction by James Allsopp

Front cover: The Cock Inn, Elkstones
Back cover top: The Cattle Market, Talbot & White Lion, Leek
Back cover bottom & page 1: The Black Lion, St Edward Street, Leek
Page 3: The Black's Head, site of Woolworths, Market Place, Leek
Opposite page: The Kings Head & Meal Market, Market Place, Leek

Dedication

This book is dedicated to the late Arthur Goldstraw of 43
Shoobridge Street, Leek, Lindsey Porter's maternal uncle. He
kindled an interest in his godson for local history and in
photography. This is the centenary year of his birth, 1905.
Most of the images here are his, although a medical
condition restricted his tipple to a soft drink.

Contents

Introduction

With the possibility of banning smoking and introducing 24-hour drinking into pubs comes the prospect of either more pub closures or just the opposite; who knows? What is clear is that whilst city centre night clubs have boomed, the traditional pubs continue to close. This book looks at a selection of pubs (not all) which have closed, changed their name or brewery, or where their surroundings have changed, but the bulk of them are pubs now lost to us. Three have closed recently – The Merrie Monk and Churnet Valley in Leek and the Queens Arms at Mayfield. The Talbot is also under threat.

Some of the text is augmented by details of dates. Most of this is from *The Victoria County History for Staffordshire, Volume 7: The Staffordshire Moorlands*. Many old inns closed at the beginning of the 20th century following a new Act of Parliament which tightened up conditions for the grant of a licence. Quite a few of these may well have opened in the 1830s when, paradoxically, there was a relaxation of licensing regulations, allowing additional pubs to open. Of those that have disappeared completely, many occur in Leek and regrettably, photographs etc of the buildings do not always survive. A remarkable exception is the fine drawing of the former Black's Head in the Market Place, Leek (see p3).

A surprise was the discovery that the old Spread Eagle Inn was not demolished in 1878 when the current Talbot was built. The latter was 'wrapped' around the older building so to speak. The rear of it may be seen to this day from the pub car park. It was an unexpected pleasure to realise this. Regrettably there are no views inside pubs in this book except for the Central Liberal Club and the well-known photograph of a horse enjoying a pint.

This book has drawn largely on the photographs in Lindsey Porter's collection, but research has been shared between father and son. We hope that this little book brings back memories (hopefully good ones), although we suspect some may be clouded by an alcoholic haze; but there is no harm in that. If you really enjoy this book, we hope you will raise a glass to 'Landlords, past and present, God bless them.'

We wish to acknowledge the assistance of Mike Greatorex, Mavis Davis, Yvonne Porter, Graham Roberts and Cathryn Walton plus those who recognise an original photograph as being theirs. Many however were taken by the late Arthur Goldstraw.

Lindsey and Phillip Porter
Ipstones and Ashbourne, 2005.

Pubs in Leek

The Abbey Inn was formerly known as The Bowling Green Inn. It was known by this name at least in 1834 and changed to The Abbey in the 1960s. After another spell as The Bowling Green, it became The Abbey for a second time. These two views show the inn as The Bowling Green and prior to the construction of the large seating area on the front. The barn is now holiday accommodation. This pub, of course, is not 'lost'. However the change of name and external alterations indicate the wider context in which 'lost' also means 'changed' so far as this book is concerned.

Above: The former Angel Inn dated 1847, in the Market Place was designed by a local firm of architects: Sugdens, who were also responsible for the Black's Head, behind the gas lamp and now occupied by Woolworths. The Angel could be the first building to be designed in Leek by William Sugden after Leek Railway Station; the first of many which still grace the town. The Angel is the middle building of the three three-storey buildings to the left of the gas lamp. It was occupied by Yates's Wine Lodge for many years along with the off-licence around the corner in Derby Street. The latter and The Angel were joined together by the main bar of Yates's. The low building on the left was replaced by the Buttermarket in 1897. It abuts The Red Lion.

Left: A close up of the pre-1847 Angel Inn – on the right of this scene and with the pointed roof.

Above: The building on the left was empty when this photo was taken in c. 1962-3. It was formerly The Beehive and has since been demolished. The buildings are on Clerk Bank and the pub was adjacent to Christopher Taylor Design. The first house on Clerk Bank (adjacent to the shop) was formerly the Horse and Jockey Inn.

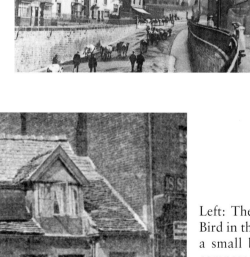

Left: The former Bird in the Hand, a small building compared to the elegant building which replaced it in 1889. The inn sign clearly gives the name. See also p6.

The rebuilt Bird in the Hand, another design by Sugdens. It bore the name Parker's Brewery on the two panels below the second-storey windows in the 1950s, and on much earlier photographs. Parker's Brewery was in Burslem and its bitter was nicknamed 'Parker's Purge'. The inn when rebuilt had a sign reading 'A Bird in the Hand is worth two in a bush' on the corner of the building. Possibly it was Parkers who rebuilt the pub. The latter of course still exists, but Parkers have gone and the inn sign has been changed several times.

Still in the Market Place, Sugdens also built this inn, the Blacks Head, one of the earliest examples of their work, dating from the 1850s. It was opened as a fancy bazaar by Woolworths in 1931. In the 18th century it was known as the Blackamoor's Head, a name which survives in Ashbourne, where The Green Man & Blackamoor's Head Royal Hotel used to have an entry in the Guinness Book of Records as the inn with the longest number of words in its name.

Left: The black and white building at the bottom of the Market Place is the inn, which was replaced by the building on page 11. It was variously known as the Buffalo's Head, Blackamoor's Head and the Black's Head. The former inn was of three bays, but the right hand bay, gabled like the two shown, is hidden. The building to the right of the inn is the former Town Hall, which had an island site at the bottom of the Market Place. This building was removed in 1871-72. Note also the earlier Angel Inn, which was replaced by 'The Angel' on p8 in 1847. The low buildings on this scene, plus the old Bird in Hand and the Kings Head and Meal Market on p34 give a good idea of how the Market Place must have looked prior to the redevelopment with replacement buildings in late Georgian-Victorian times. See also p3.

Below: The Black Lion Inn on the corner of Strangman Street and St Edward Street. It was removed to widen the junction when Strangman Street was laid out in 1887-88 on Strangman Walk. The inn was replaced by the former Post Office, which in turn was demolished for a much larger development for the GPO in c. 1963.

Above: The Black Swan, Sheep Market, taken in the early 1960s. Actually, the front has hardly changed but it is hidden now behind window blinds and lots of flowers.

Below: A view of the Blue Ball Inn taken in the early 1960s. It was situated adjacent to a former Co-op shop. Both buildings were demolished for road widening purposes a short time later. The Co-op shop was adjacent to the motor repair garage below the former Ragged School.

Above: A 1950s view of the Blue Ball Inn, Mill Street.

Below: This scene of The Britannia in West Street shows little change so far as the pub is concerned. We included it because it shows the adjacent houses, which were pulled down in the 1960s. The three-storey building and those beyond it occupied the site of the current car park. Demolition also allowed extensions on two sides of the pub. Adjacent Belle Vue was set out at 36 feet wide in 1891-92. The old pub sign looks far better than many today. It is time they were brought back.

Above: It would have been difficult to have left this one out! It captured high jinks at the Central Liberal Club in Market Street at the time of the 1953 Coronation. This is another Sugden building, typically three-storey and with lots of character. The Club is still there of course, but the horse has long gone!

Below: The Cheshire Cheese Inn on the corner of Sheep Market and St Edward Street. It was also a hotel. Prior to being called by this name, the pub was known as the Coach and Horses. It was a pub at the beginning of the 19th century. The three-storey building on the extreme left is The George Hotel, demolished to widen Church Street (see p25-27).

Above: The former Cock Inn at the top of the Market Place, prior to being rebuilt. It was probably the oldest delicensed pub in the town. It had closed its doors by the 1820s. The pavement on this side of the Market Place was not laid down until 1888-89. The name of the old Cock Inn survived with the later Cock Inn lower down the row of buildings.

Left: This Cock Inn to the right of Baskerville's was adjacent to the Red Lion Hotel in the Market Place. It is now occupied by two shops.

Above: Here is another view from coaching days of the Cock Inn (it only closed recently).

Below: Another Cock Inn, in Derby Street. This inn dates from the early 19th century. It has been one of the focal points of town life since then, especially upon Market days. The inn remains to this day, of course, and this scene is included to recall the past times when coaches left from here and at the Duke of York as well as the Roebuck. The coach is loaded with baskets and one wonders if someone was 'doing the shopping' for a local village. See also p27 for more on coaching inns in Leek.

G. & J. MUNRO & Co., Ltd.,

WHOLESALE & RETAIL

WINE, SPIRIT,

Ale & Porter Merchants,

DERBY STREET, LEEK, and

MARKET STREET, HANLEY.

SOLE AGENTS FOR

OLD GAUL,

"X X X,"

" RESERVE,"

"LIQUEUR,"

GREER'S O. V. H. WHISKY.

GOODS DELIVERED FREE TO ALL PARTS.

The Cock Inn, in Derby Street was also the initial outlet for G & J Munroe, when John Munroe was the landlord. The firm of Munroes, wine and spirit merchants, later occupied the double fronted property below The Valiant, formerly the Queen's Head in Stanley Street. Here is an advert for the firm when it was based at The Cock.

Above: The white painted shop (Cumberlidge's millinery shop) in Church Street and the one to the right of it (see p26) butted up to the rear of The George Hotel and once formed part of the hotel. The stone-faced building next was the Conservative Club, built on the site of The Crown Inn. The street was demolished for road widening in 1972.

Below: At the bottom of Mill Street is the Conservative Working Men's Club. Cottages adjacent to it were demolished in the 1960s and are shown on this view. The Club, established in 1912, was The Spread Eagle in the 19th century. It was thought that the building which had existed to the right of the cottages may have belonged to the last abbot, or was that a story kept until close to closing time?

Opposite page top: Separated from the Golden Lion Inn by an archway, was the King William IV. The latter closed c.1908-12.

Opposite page bottom: The Cross Keys Inn in Stanley Street. This was later a site occupied by The Bazaar. Two crossed keys may just be seen on the inn-sign.

The Dog and Partridge Inn, formerly at 11 Derby Street. Mention elsewhere is made of buildings designed by the Sugdens. W. Sugden & Son occupied the premises to the right of the inn. Sugden's house is now Boots the Chemist. The pub site has recently been redeveloped with two new shops – one being W.H. Smith & Son.

Left: 'Tub Thumper' Deakin's cooperage in Derby Street, Leek. This was not a pub but a cooperage which made barrels for the beer trade. This was in Derby Street in the premises now occupied by Graingers. Deakins also sold yokes etc as may be seen. The owner of the business was known as 'Tub Thumper' Deakin, no doubt from his occupation of making barrels.

Below: The Duke of York, a Marston's house in Derby Street, closed in April 1961 and was pulled down to make way for Fine Fare's supermarket. The site is now occupied by the Leek United Building Society. Two stalls occupied the cobbled forecourt on market days. It is now covered over, but is still open fronted.

Above: It is known that the pub was the headquarters of Leek Cyclists. Here they are seen together, probably at a carnival or something similar. The sign on the bike in the centre says 'Royal Wellington Road Racer Beats the World'. The cock on the right sits on a bike with two signs saying 'Royal Wellington Cycles, Cock of the Walk'. Somebody had an eye to marketing 100 or so years ago!

Below: The last photo, at the Duke of York, is of the Buxton coach about to depart from outside the inn. It was taken in 1895.

The Dun Cow Inn in Court No 7 on Ashbourne Road (formerly London Road, on Leek Moor), overshadowed by Brough's London Mill. It was a pub and lodging house and was demolished by Broughs in the 1950s. The passageway ran through to Cross Street.

Above: The Dyers Arms at Low Hamil, the area between Mill Street and Bridge End, now Macclesfield Road. Formerly a Bass House, this photograph was taken in the early 1960s prior to the demolition of the adjacent houses.

Below: The George Hotel, situated on the corner of St Edward Street and Church Street until 1972 when it was demolished for road widening. It was a Georgian coaching inn, probably built c. 1760. The Jazz Club used to meet here until forced to relocate.

25

Two views of The George Hotel. Below shows the view of the Swan Hotel, still going strong and the oldest pub in the town. It was formerly the Swan with Two Necks and prior to that it was the George and Dragon.

The George Hotel and adjacent properties in St Edward Street. Most of the site is now a car park opposite The Swan Inn. The London-Manchester coach stopped here, while others on the same route stopped at the Swan, which was opposite. Quite a few pubs in the town enhanced their income by attracting through traffic. The Wilkes's Head did so, with the Manchester-Birmingham coach; the Duke of York was a terminus for the Leek-Buxton coach; The Earl of Shrewsbury's coach between Alton Towers, Cheadle, Leek and Buxton used The Red Lion; The Roe Buck – built in 1627 – and The Red Lion handled Manchester, Birmingham and London traffic while several other inns shown in this book have coaches parked outside, no doubt handling more local traffic.

The Globe Inn in St Edward's Street. It was demolished to make way for High Street. This occurred after the sale of The Field estate. This former large house, built in Georgian times on the edge of Leek, still exists as the National Reserve Club. High Street, Field Street and Salisbury Street were laid out on the former estate in 1904. Next to The Globe was Flallon's buchery and above it stands Parr's Bank, now Bank House. It was the site of The Old Plough.

Above: Another view of The Globe Inn. The sign over the bay window reads 'Shallcross' and the window is full of bottles. The licensee was George H. Bowyer and Mrs Shallcross ran a separate business, an off-licence.

Below: The Golden Lion in Church Street. It existed in 1786 and may have been in existence in 1756. Like The George Hotel and the properties in between, it was demolished in 1972. This scene shows people alighting from a coach, with their bags and baggage. With the trees, cobbles and gas lamp, it is an evocative scene.

Left: A captivating view of a cart in the yard at the rear of the Golden Lion. One of the buildings in the yard – probably the one seen – was a theatre in the late 18th century. It was known as the Long Room or Play Room. A century later, there was a blacksmith here.

Below: The Golden Lion shortly before demolition.

Opposite page: The Grapes Vaults at 31a St Edward Street. It was two doors up from the Bull's Head, which of course is still open. When this photograph was taken it was The Grapes and Goodwill Vaults. It is now Leek Signs and Graphics.

Two views of the Kings Arms, an Ind Coope house. The pub existed in 1837 and was probably named after one of the George's. When Mill Street was widened, it was one of the few places to have survived (another was the former Nag's Head, opposite). It was, until recently, The Jester and incorporated the adjacent cottage. Behind is Big Mill, built in 1857.

The premises are (at the time of writing) being refurbished, but not as a pub.

Above: The Lord Raglan Inn occupied the corner of Brook Street and Compton, opposite the Unicorn Inn (see p43). It was demolished as part of a street widening programme, which saw the removal of all the properties on the left side of the bottom of Compton, c. 1912. It is the property on the extreme left. The cellars were used as underground toilets for many years but have now been abandoned. The event looks like the annual Club Day procession, perhaps of All Saints or St Mary's heading for the Market Place. Lord Raglan gave the order for the Charge of the Light Brigade during the Crimean War, on 24th October, 1854.

Below: The Moss Rose Inn on the edge of town at the corner of Buxton Road and Moss Rose Lane. Today it has not changed too much and of course, is still open. It has lost all the ivy now. The guide post at the junction used to give the direction and distance to Leek Railway Station: $1^1/_4$ miles.

Above & Below: This old building was in Leek Market Place, close to the Bird in Hand. It was the Meal Market and Kings Head Inn. Mathew Miller's *Olde Leeke, Volume 1* states that a wife was sold here for 1s 9d (8³/₄p)! There is little information available on this inn, but it clearly was one of several low buildings which bordered the Market Place. It features on the top left-hand corner of the view below. Its signboard reading 'Kings Head' may be seen on p12. The current building is the Cancer Research shop.

Above: This building is currently empty having been an antique shop. For years it was Ron Deaville's motor cycle shop. It used to be the Nags Head Inn at 120 Mill Street, but now stands proud of adjacent properties. The other scene (inset) shows how it used to appear. It's the white building halfway down on the right.

Below: The Pig and Whistle which stood on the corner of Osborne Street and Buxton road. It was later called The Hanging Gate, which name it possessed in 1837.

Above left: The Queen's Head, Stanley Street, although the name is hidden by the snow! Several pubs have changed names: The Weaver's Arms is now the White Lion; The Union in Stockwell Street is Benks; the Queens Arms (see top right) is the Blue Mugge; The Bowling Green is The Abbey and there are doubtless others in the area. This photograph portrays a lost kind of transport once common everywhere.

Above right: The Queen's Arms, now the Blue Mugge and much extended into a popular hostelry.

Below: Contrasting with the above scene, this shows much activity outside The Railway Tavern in Broad Street, now demolished and the site of a car showroom.

The Railway Tavern, seen here with neighbouring properties and the bottom of Sneyd Street (left).

The Roe Buck in Derby Street is of course a popular hostelry, but the removal of Tatton's Confectioners next door revealed the timber framing on the east side of the inn for a while (see next page). Here is the pub prior to the demolition work next door.

Above: This view shows differences in the ground floor windows and is probably taken prior to the photograph on p37.

Left: Side view of the Roe Buck following the demolition of Tatton's Cake & Bread shop. The wooden framing is now hidden again.

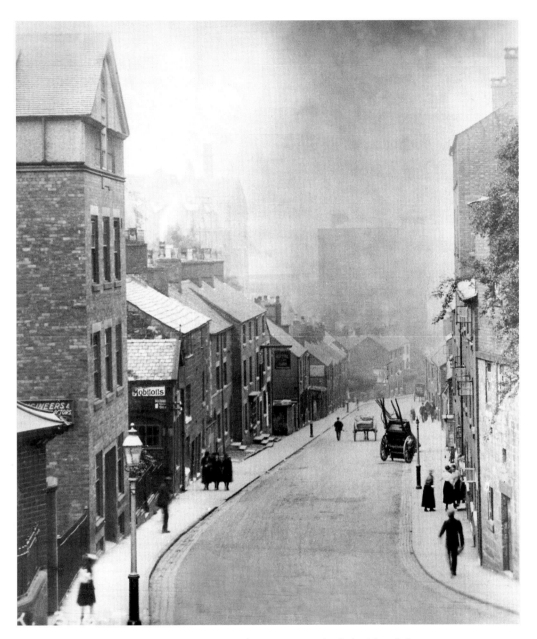

The Royal Oak Inn, Mill Street, seen with its sign on the left side of the street.

Above: The site of the Royal Oak (with the whitewashed rear walls being the rock face) adjacent to Donkey Bank steps.

Below: Perhaps the most unusual photograph in the book: a performing bear outside the Sea Lion in Russell Street. (However the 'bear's' feet look remarkably like human feet!).
The end part of the pub was removed to 'iron-out' a kink where Brook Street met Haywood Street and the door was placed across the corner of the building. To maintain the size of the pub, the adjacent house was incorporated into the part remaining. Brook Street was

widened between 1874 and 1882 to a width of 36 feet, but the pub scheme may have been later. Russell Street was created when the Black Lion Inn in Derby Street was de-molished and the street laid down across gardens etc at the rear. The latter was a low building like the Old Angel and Bird in the Hand nearby.

Above: The Southbank Hotel, Southbank, Leek. It became The Mulberry in 1964 and was demolished in 2001. It was the main establishment in the town for social gatherings for decades. The site and the former garden (later a car park) has now been developed with houses.

Below: The Spread Eagle Inn, replaced by The Talbot at the bottom of Ashbourne Road. In c. 1854, a man sold his wife for a quart of ale here (Miller's *Olde Leeke*, Vol I). The purchaser, an Irish binding weaver, reckoned he did very well from the deal too. The name Spread Eagle had been changed to Talbot by 1837. The current building is dated 1878 but the building shown here was not demolished. It can be clearly seen from the car park at the rear (See p42)! The new extensions adjoined the front and the road frontages. The inn sign was of a large dog (a Talbot) with 'a nice curly tail'.

Above: A landlord's dream come true! The inn in the background is The Talbot Hotel, another Sugden building. The crowd is not queuing to get into the pub; it's the Golden Jubilee celebrations of June 1887. It is difficult to imagine the landlord not having another reason to celebrate for all that. Until a few years ago, this was a Higson's Brewery tied house. The 1887 celebrations started with an ox roast in the Market Place and also included the opening of Pickwood Recreation Ground that day, when 5,000 scholars were presented with a commemorative mug.

Below: The Wheatsheaf in St Edward Street, on the corner of Stanley Street. Another

design by Sugdens, unfortunately now without the top storey. After being a bookmaker's for many years, it reopened as a pub: the Den Engel (The Angel), selling Belgian beers and it is now the Hydr 8 bar. The Wheatsheaf is re-puted to have had the longest bar in Leek. Den Engel are now at Munroe's Wine shop in Stanley Street (See p18).

Above: The Wilkes's Head is of course still open, but its sign has changed. This gave a little more detail on John Wilkes, whose outspoken views in his newspaper upset the King, causing Wilkes to flee abroad for his own safety. He was cross-eyed and this isn't too apparent on the current sign. There are only a handful of inns carrying Wilkes's name, despite being a pioneer in establishing the right to free speech. The former bank next door was built on the site of a pub: The Old Plough (see also p28). Wilkes's Head was a Parker's tied house when this scene was taken in the early 1960s but prior to 1963, when properties further down were demolished for the Post Office. Westminster Bank succeeded Parr's Bank.

Below: The Unicorn at the corner of St Edward Street and Brook Street. These premises were demolished to make way for the current building and this scene probably records the start of the demolition work in 1897. The Quiet Woman next door remains largely as shown here.

In addition to alcohol, the pubs also sold ginger beer, as they still do. This was made in Leek by George Massey and his son Richard, in premises off Leonard Street. Access was via the lower of the two arches on this scene. 'Pop' Massey's cart is outside the arch. His bottles were made by Kilner and had a marble stopper. They were endorsed 'Massey' and 'Leek'. Two are shown in the lower photograph. The business closed in the 1930s after at least 50 years trading.

WALKER'S LEEK BREWERY.

 ## Pale, Mild & Bitter Ales and Stout

Absolutely Pure. Always in Condition.

In 4½, 6, 9, 10, 12, or 18 GALLON CASKS,

At Special Low Prices for Cash.

IRISH & SCOTCH WHISKY & RUMS,

From 2/6 per Bottle.

GINS at 2/-, 2/6 and 3/- per Bottle.
BRANDIES from 2/10   „   „
WINES   „   1/6   „   „

All the leading brands of 'Special' Whiskies.

Over 50 years' reputation for purity and excellence of quality.   —   —

☞ ASK FOR PRICE LISTS.

One of the area's brewers was Walkers, in business in 1834 and still going strong in 1911. It was situated on the corner of Broad Street and Alsop Street.

Recently closed pubs. Above: The Churnet Valley, Newcastle Road.

Below: The Merrie Monk (formerly The Green Man Inn), Compton, now a B&B called The Green Man.

Pubs in the Staffordshire Moorlands

In this section, each village name is given first

BRADNOP
Above: The Blacksmiths Arms. This inn was situated on the crossroads on the Leek-Ashbourne Road and existed in c. 1850. It was recorded in this scene after being destroyed by fire in c. 1940. The building was rebuilt. You can see the inn sign, badly scorched, portraying an anvil and the name of the licensee: Plant.

BUTTERTON
Below: The former Red Lion Inn occupied this building.

Above: The Black Lion Inn, looking as it was built, as an inn and with a stable attached. In 1973 it was redeveloped with a large extension behind the stable and with sensitive internal refurbishment, by Geoffrey and Elizabeth Cox. The previous landlord, George Goodwin, sold all his beer direct from the barrel off a stillage at the rear of the right hand room.

CHEDDLETON

Below: This is the Red Lion, still open of course, although this view of it has changed a lot. The petrol pump, one of the two shops and the forge have all gone.

Above: Cheddleton had its own brewery and it also bottled Guinness stout. A bottle of the latter (empty) was displayed at the Nicholson Institute for many years. The brewery was in the two-storey building to the right of the bridge.

ELKSTONES
Right: A group photo-graph outside the Cock Inn. It was serving ale in 1816 and closed in 1976. John Bradbury was the landlord when this photo-graph was taken. The vil-lage pump was across the road from the inn and a few yards down the road. No doubt the girl with the yoke was going there next.

Above: The Cock in c. 1963, when Redvers Cooper was the landlord. The bar was in the room to the right of the door.

ELLASTONE

Below: The Bromley Arms, a Worthington house, in c. 1960. It was named after the Bromley Davenports who owned nearby Wootton Hall, demolished in 1935. The former inn is now a private dwelling. The other building in the scene is the Duncombe Arms (formerly a Bass Brewery house), still there, named after the owners of Calwich Abbey which was also demolished in 1935. Presumably this closed when Bass took over Worthington's Brewery.

FROGHALL

Above: The Navigation Inn, photographed when derelict in 1974. It was above the portal to the canal at Froghall. It may well have been built before the tunnel, when the canal ended at this point. The tunnel was built in 1785.

GRINDON

Below: The inn sign reads Shoulder of Mutton, but little has changed externally. The name has though, for nearly forty years or so it has been The Cavalier.

HULME END

Above: Some pubs keep the same name for centuries and others seem to keep changing. This popular inn was erected adjacent to a new bridge by the new turnpike road from Onecote and Warslow through Hartington to Newhaven. It was called the Jolly Carter by 1834 but within a few years had become the Waggon and Horses, certainly by 1850. After reverting to the Jolly Carter, it was the Hulme End Inn by 1879. Shortly into the new century, the Manifold Valley Railway opened (1904) and the inn became the Light Railway Hotel. Possibly the extension was built at this time. In the early 1980s it became the Manifold Valley Hotel and it's now the Manifold Valley Inn. That's six names! This scene was taken before the restaurant was added, when it was the Hulme End Inn. It is now a popular Inn, eating house and provider of rooms, self catering and camping accommodation. Diversification must be the route to survival for many rural pubs.

IPSTONES

Right: This was the Red Lion on Ipstones Edge, now a dwellinghouse. It closed in 1966 and was a Joules Brewery (of Stone, Staffs) house. There is a good description of life at this pub in *Ipstones Revealed in Memories*, describing days gone by when many rural pubs combined pub-keeping and farming. There are not many of them left these days.

52

Ipstones still has four pubs: The Red Lion; the Marquis of Granby; the Sea Lion; and what was the Golden Lion (now the Linden Tree). The last three were Joules' Brewery houses and the Red Lion, a Burtonwood house. These two pubs (the Marquis above and the [now] Linden Tree below) are shown to recall a good brewery lost when it was taken over by Bass. The Linden Tree fronts the main road through the village, now a busy highway, but making less impact in Edwardian times when the photograph was probably taken. The name changed in the late 1980s. It was built in 1838 and the landlord below is Samuel Barker.

Above: Not in Ipstones, but at the far end of Ipstones Edge, was the Green Man at Windy Arbour. It closed about a decade ago.

LONGNOR

LONGNOR

Opposite page bottom/this page/following page top: On 24th September 1831, there was much activity in the Market Place as a bull was baited – one of the last years in which it would have occurred (Ashbourne being one of the last places where it occurred in England, over a decade later). These views show The Cheshire Cheese (below and on p56), and above, in the Market Place, The Crewe and Harpur Arms, both in bygone days. Note the building restricting the width of the road outside the Cheshire Cheese Inn on p56.

LONGNOR

MAYFIELD

Below: A view of the Queens Arms at Mayfield, by the former narrow road bridge before it was widened. The old bridge witnessed many road accidents as vehicles came to grief through brake failure or excessive speed. Staffordshire pubs used to close at 10.30pm whilst the Royal Oak at the opposite end of the bridge shut at 11.00, being in Derbyshire. Until comparatively recently, the Oak had an influx of drinkers by 10.45pm who crossed the bridge for another pint! In 2004 the Queens Arms was converted to six apartments. They were put up for sale in March 2005.

MEERBROOK

Above: The Three Horseshoes Inn, now The Lazy Trout. Three horse shoes can be seen as the inn sign on the extreme right. This inn was here in 1818 (as The Horseshoe). It was the Three Horseshoes in 1834. This was taken in the early 1960s when Ernest Belfield was the licensee.

Below & following page top: Two views of The Fountain Inn, formerly situated down the lane to the right of Three Horseshoes. It was demolished c. 1962 when Tittesworth Reservoir was extended. This inn existed in 1834 under the same name. The two gentlemen are Norman Plant (left) and Vic Porter (right), both of Leek. It was an Ind Coope house.

MEERBROOK

OAKAMOOR

Below: The Admiral Jervis in Oakamoor. This inn probably became delicensed prior to 1868 when the Oakamoor Mills chaplain began services there. The year later, a Reading Room was in use there. (Details from the Diary of A S Bolton). A Coffee House also opened adjacent to this building. In 1971, its licence was restored, after a break of over 100 years.

RUDYARD

Above: The Rudyard Hotel. This photograph dates from 1868, prior to alterations to both the building and the grounds, and the name – changed to Hotel Rudyard in c. 1886. It had opened in 1851.

Below: The former Station Hotel, currently closed as a Public House. It's a sad situation in which to find a once fine and popular pub. It was later called The New Galleon.

SWAINSLEY

Above: Swainsley Hall, in the Manifold Valley. Built in 1864, by Richard Roscoe, a London solicitor, it became a pub in the 1950s, run by the late Doug Blackhurst, who also established Belle Engineering at Sheen, manufacturing concrete mixers. It reverted to a dwelling a few years later but became a restaurant in the 1980s. It is now a dwelling again.

UPPER HULME

Left: A view of the Royal Cottage at Middle Hills, on the Leek-Buxton road. It shows a feature which does not survive: the mounting block (beneath the ladder). What appear to be seats maybe seen on a Victorian etching to the left of the door (See below).

WARSLOW

Above: The former Grouse Inn at Warslow. It probably had this name from October 1853 when Izaac Birch became the landlord. It had previously been called The Crewe and Harpur Arms, after the Harpur Crewe family who owned Warslow Hall. The Inn became a temperance establishment between 1900 and 1904. Ecton Lee at Swainsley became another with the opening of the Manifold Valley Light Railway in 1904. It is held locally that the latter, despite its alcohol-free aspirations, could also supply a drop of gin at the back door!

WATERHOUSES

Below: The George Inn survives in Waterhouses and is gaining a good reputation for its fish dishes. It follows the Olde Beams Restaurant, now closed, which was also well known for its food. The latter occupied the former site of The George Inn, shown here with its name sign on the far side of the road. The building is now a dwelling and the barn on the extreme right has been removed. The Olde Beams closed in 2002. Presumably the building ceased to be a pub when the licence was transferred to the current pub.

Inns & Public Houses in Leek in the year 1837

COMMERCIAL HOTELS

George	T. Tatler	Spout Street
Red Lion	J. Barlow	Market Place
Roe Buck	J. Lowndes	Derby Street
Swan	W. Gorman	Spout Street

INNS

Angel	Martha Smith	Market Place
Ball Haye Tavern	W. Davenport	Ball Haye Green
Bird in Hand	B. White	Market Place
Black's Head	Joseph Chell	Custard Street
Black Swan	Thomas Gascoigne	Sheep Market
Blue Ball	Jonathon Plant	Mill Street
Bull's Head	Thomas Hine	Spout Street
Butcher's Arms *	John Chapell	Derby Street
Cheshire Cheese	Thomas West	Sheep Market
Cock	William Glover	Market Place
Cock	Samuel Lasseter	Derby Place
Cross Keys	G. Critchlow	Custard Street
Crown	Isaac Hammond	Church Street
Dog and Partridge	Joseph Perkin	Derby Street
Duke of York	Jonathon Jackson	Derby Street
Fountain	Sarah Kirkham	Fountain Street
Globe	Vernon Hulme	Spout Street
Golden Lion	T. Hulme	Church Street
King's Arms	Ely Plant	Mill Street
King's Head *	Joseph Walker	Market Place
Nag's Head	William Rider	Mill Street
Old Plough *	John Leese	Spout Street
Queen's Head	George Walker	Custard Street
Quiet Woman	John Maskery	Spout Street
Royal Oak	Elizabeth Dale	Buxton Road
Spotted Cow *	Peter Swindells	Leek Moor
Talbot	R. Ratcliffe	Leek Moor
Unicorn	William Mellor	Spout Street
Union	R. Hawksworth	Stockwell Street
Weaver's Arms *	T. Johnson	Leek Moor
White Lion	John Hawkins	Bridge End
Wilkes's Head	Joseph Pickford	Spout Street
William IV	John Hulme	Church Street

* Closed by 1887, but the Spotted Cow had become the Dun Cow and the Weaver's Arms the White Lion. Established between 1837 and 1887 were: The Cattle Market, Churnet Valley, Grapes and Sea Lion.

Beer Houses in Leek in the Year 1837

Albion	T. Robinson	Spout Street
Bee Hive	U. Davenport	Clerk's Bank
Blue Bell	J. Williamson	Buxton Road
Britannia	W. Alcock	Spout Street Square
Coach & Horses	George Gould	Derby Street
Crispin's Arms	John Heavy	Mill Street
Earl Grey	John Goodall	Leek Moor
Flying Horse	Edward Allen	Ashbourne Road
Green Dragon	Job Allbank	Spout Street
Hanging Gate	William Dawson	Buxton Road
Horse and Jockey	George Caley	Clerk's Bank
Marquis of Granby	Mr Hirst	Mill Street
Mason's Arms	Vernon Fogg	Workhouse Street
Nag's Head	R. Murfin	Stockwell Street
Malster's Arms (Maltshovel)		
	R. Mellor	Spooner's Lane
New Inn	B. Wilson	Buxton Road
Navigation	J. McCormick	Spooner's Lane
Pump	Thomas Clowes	Mill Street
Rising Sun	H. Goodwin	King Street
Royal Compass	I. Heath	London Row
True Blue	R. Smith	Mill Street
Vine	J. Phillips	King Street
White Hart	John Gilman	Stockwell Street

Wine and Spirits Vaults

One each connected with:

Crown	Church Street
William IV	Church Street
Old Plough	Spout Street
Wilkes's Head	Spout Street
Spread Eagle	Leek Moor

Old Streets Re-named:

From	**To**
Back Sides	Pickwood Road
Barn Gates	West Street
Cope's Yard	Getliffe's Yard
Custard Street	Stanley Street
Leek Moor	Ashbourne Road
London Row	London Street
Newtown	King Street
Nix Hill	Wellington Street
Spooners Lane & Canal Street	Broad Street
Spout Street	St Edward Street
Workhouse Street	Brook Street

(Detail from Miller's *Leek 50 Years Ago*)

LANDMARK COLLECTOR'S LIBRARY

HISTORY OF THE ANCIENT PARISH OF LEEK (1884)

John Sleigh

A limited-run new edition of this fascinating and sought after book (the enlarged edition). This edition also includes the text of a lecture by William Challinor on the author and his book, plus an etching of the author. It also has four colour plates of family crests etc. It includes quite a few family trees, of interest to family researchers.

Specification: 288pp plus 4 pages in colour; 304 x 248mm; hardback sewn binding; 3000 micron board cover with newvap gold lettering to spine and front (no jacket).
PRICE: £50.00

LOST HOUSES OF NORTH STAFFORDSHIRE

Cathryn Walton and Lindsey Porter

From the authors of 'Spirit of Leek, Volumes 1, 2 & 3' and 'Staffordshire Moorlands & the Churnet Valley'.

A study of approximately 50 houses, most demolished and some now changed or enjoying a different use. Many were country seats, but some town houses are included. This is a pictorial study, supported by historical text in most cases.

Specification: Approx 160pp and 100 illustrations; 246 x 172mm; hardback
ISBN: 1-84306-195-3
PRICE: £19.99

THE SPIRIT OF LEEK: VOLUME 4

Cathryn Walton

A follow up to 'Spirit of Leek, Volumes 1, 2 & 3'

A look at past times, events and personalities in Leek, illustrated with old and new photographs.

Details upon request.

Landmark Publishing Ltd
Ashbourne Hall, Cokayne Ave, Ashbourne, Derbyshire DE6 1EJ England
Tel: (01335) 347349 Fax: (01335) 347303
e-mail: landmark@clara.net web site: www.landmarkpublishing.co.uk